50
Famous Fables
and Folk Tales
Collected from Around the World

Retold by
TOM BAKER

Schiffer Publishing Ltd

4880 Lower Valley Road · Atglen, PA 19310

Library of Congress Control Number: 2016951297

Designed by Brenda McCallum
Cover design by Brenda McCallum
Type set in Bodoni MT/Janda Elegant Handwritting

ISBN: 978-0-7643-5197-6
Printed in China

Published by Schiffer Publishing, Ltd.
4880 Lower Valley Road
Atglen, PA 19310
Phone: (610) 593-1777; Fax: (610) 593-2002
E-mail: Info@schifferbooks.com
Web: www.schifferbooks.com

For our complete selection of fine books on this and related
subjects, please visit our website at www.schifferbooks.com.
You may also write for a free catalog.

Schiffer Publishing's titles are available at special discounts
for bulk purchases for sales promotions or premiums. Special
editions, including personalized covers, corporate imprints, and
excerpts, can be created in large quantities for special needs.
For more information, contact the publisher.

We are always looking for people to write books on new and
related subjects. If you have an idea for a book, please contact us
at proposals@schifferbooks.com.

Dedicated to all readers and storytellers, everywhere!

Acknowledgments

Special thanks to Dinah Roseberry and Schiffer Books,
to my family, to my mother Brenda Durham, and to everyone
else who has supported my creative work over the years.
Warmest regards!

Contents

Introduction

A fable can be loosely defined as a story, usually involving talking animals (in much the same way as newspaper comics), in which a moral or lesson is imparted. These stories have been handed down and collected for centuries, but their essential truths remain the same: they are pearls of wisdom, nuggets of meaning meant to instruct and impart truths to the young and the impressionable.

The most famous collection of these timeless tales are attributed to the Greek slave Aesop (620–564 BCE), who was described as being monstrously ugly, perhaps deformed, and eventually won his freedom. He was the adviser to kings and the dinner companion of the Seven Sages before being thrown from a cliff by a crowd of angry Delphians (why they were so angry at him is not made clear). The Delphians, for their part, suffered pestilence and plague afterward. So ended the illustrious career of the supposed sage.

Of course, none of this can be conclusively proven to have ever actually occurred. However, the fables, whether written and collected by the ill-fated and ugly Aesop, or by another who simply used his identity, still retain the essential truths that have made them immortal yarns. They are as important today as they were a thousand years ago, teaching the same lessons.

We have liberally dipped into the fables of several divergent cultures, including Hindu, Indian, African, Chinese, Native American, as well as fables generally French, Russian, British, etc. All of these different cultures have their own traditions, and their own special wisdom. Their stories each have their own special appeal. A few of these stories, though, are not traditional fables; we have also included folktales that have a more open-ended meaning to them, or no real readymade moral. There are a few tales that rely more on magic than others, and stretch back thousands of years in their respective cultures.

Now, enjoy! And don't forget to learn something along the way!

To Kill a Killer!

Once, long ago, a man murdered a friend—seemingly for no other reason than that the friend owed him a little money and he couldn't repay it. The family of the man he murdered soon found out about his villainy and, putting together a posse, chased the man across the craggy earth until they came to a vast, rushing river.

The murderer, who was somewhat ahead of the mob pursuing him, spied a lion drinking at the river. Panicked, for he knew the lion would kill him just as surely as the vigilantes chasing him, he quickly climbed into the branches of a tree. He hid amidst the verdant green leaves, wiping sweat from his brow.

All at once, he began to hear a slithering and a hissing near his leg and, looking down, spied a long, twisty serpent climbing steadily toward him up the trunk of the tree. He felt his grip on the branches slip as he reeled in terror. Suddenly, he was falling!

He fell with a great splash into the river, and, being an excellent swimmer, thought he had finally found his means of escape. He paddled furiously and happily, then realized he had come to the most terrible climax of his short, violent life! For there was an immense crocodile stalking him! It slowly crept toward him as he began to furiously swim toward shore. Alas, he was not quite quick enough!

Later, as the avengers gathered at the bank of the river to watch the crocodile finish his bloody feast, one of them reflected, "Thus, it proves what I have always known: the earth, the air, and the water alike will all refuse to shelter a killer."

What you do will always come back to haunt you!

(Source: Aesop)

The Foolish Man and the Fiery Ants

Once there was a wise old man walking along the coast, watching as a ship seemed to flounder and then sink beneath the waves.

Realizing this meant the death of many, if not all of those on board, the wise old man fell to his knees and beat his breast, cursing God that He was so unjust as "to kill a shipload of innocent people for the sake of, most likely, killing *one* guilty man!"

Suddenly, the man cried out in pain, and, jumping to his feet, realized he had fallen right on top of an army of fiery ants. He began to stomp and thrash in pain and anger, squashing the innocent ants until there were none that were left alive.

The man was about to jump into the surf to wash his bleeding knees when, in a flash of light, a strange man with winged sandals appeared before him. It was Mercury.

Mercury pointed his weird, serpent-shaped staff at the man, and asked, "Who are you to curse God for *His* ways, when you've dealt with these ants in the same manner?"

Alway treat others the way YOU want to be treated.

(Source: Aesop)

3

The Thief and the Innkeeper

Once upon a time a lowly thief decided he must steal something from a rather stupid, oafish innkeeper.

He quickly paid the last of his small pittance of money to the innkeeper and rented a room. Then he watched carefully, day after day, for anything the innkeeper might own that he could easily steal.

He watched and waited until, one day, he saw that the innkeeper had acquired a fine new coat, which he coveted greatly. He devised a plan on how he might separate the innkeeper from this particular article of clothing without too much risk or danger to himself.

One day, when he was sitting by the fire warming himself, the thief saw the innkeeper come in wearing the coat and he bade him come quickly and sit with him. The innkeeper huffed and puffed and sighed, but he did as his guest requested, making sure to take off his fine coat and lay it on the back of his chair.

The thief suddenly yawned. And then, most mysteriously, began to howl like a wolf!

The innkeeper found himself slightly alarmed, and asked his guest, "Why do you howl like that?"

The thief replied, "Sir, it is because, when I have yawned three times, I turn into a vicious werewolf, and kill whoever I can lay hands upon!" And having said that, the thief yawned once more.

The innkeeper suddenly felt panicked and, getting up, looked as if he were about to bolt for the door.

The thief proceeded to divest himself of his outer garments—vest, shirt, stockings—saying, "No sir, I beg you, please hold onto my clothing, as I shall surely rip them when I finish my transformation into a terrible wolf!" And he yawned a third time and sent up such a howling din it must have been heard all across the village, and perhaps, across the countryside.

The innkeeper shouted and fled in terror. The thief stopped howling and started laughing. He quickly donned his clothes again, snatched up the innkeeper's coat, and was out the door, never to be seen in that village again.

And the moral of this story is: One should not ALWAYS believe everything one is told.

(Source: Aesop)

The Green Jackass

(We can be forgiven for considering the following tale as being somewhat pointless. It is, however, still amusing.)

Once, in Germany, long ago, a simple soul decided to test the credulity of his fellow villagers. He took his old donkey, and, leading him out to the field, got his green and red paint cans and set to work. Soon, he had a most exotic-looking animal: a jackass that was green with bright red legs.

That next morning, he took pleasure in leading the strange animal through the village square, where it quickly became a cause of some sensation and comment. The other villagers exclaimed that the simple soul (who passed for the village idiot) must have been blessed by God to find such a rare, wonderful creature.

It was not long before the idiot (or so he was always thought of by his neighbors) had secured the donkey in a wooden booth, and was charging a small admission price to come in and examine him. Thus, his strange ruse became profitable.

The story tells us that the novelty soon wore off, however. We can assume the village idiot found himself back at square one.

(Source: Germany)

5

The King Who Inspired Courage

There once were two kingdoms: one of vast wealth and the other of comparatively little wealth. The wealthy kingdom was perpetually at war with the poorer one, the ruler of which was forever plotting with his advisers how he might get the upper hand against his rich enemy.

Well, once, when the situation had reached a boiling point, the king of the poor kingdom learned that his wealthy neighbor was finally marching against him to settle matters once and for all. Alarmed, he sent ahead a spy to wait on the ridge overlooking the valley.

The spy hid amidst the brush at the top of the ridge. He started to get out his spy glass when, suddenly, struck by a bright flash of light some miles away, he soon realized he would hardly need it. His jaw fell open, and he quickly turned and rode back to the king.

The king asked him to size up the situation, and the spy replied, "Sire! Today, we may well be attacked by an army representing a vast fortune. For, I saw so many lances that the number of them could well blot out the sun!"

At this, the noble ruler rent his garment and fell to the floor. Then, getting up, he turned to his advisers and said, "If it pleases God, today we will fight in the shadow cast by our enemies' lances!"

And it was by these famous words the old ruler inspired his people to win the war.

*Never give up, no matter what the odds
are against you!*

(Source: French)

6

The Woman and the Snake

"Thou Shalt Not Nurse a Viper!" should be the Eleventh Commandment.

Or, put it another way: Once, there was an old woman who lived in a house on the edge of a vast wilderness. One day, when she was going to the well to fetch a pail of water, she came upon a snake. It was twisted in the grass, and was quite obviously injured.

The woman said to herself: "I'll take this little one home and nurse it back to health. Maybe then I won't be so confounded lonely anymore."

And so she took the snake home, and fed it on fresh milk, and soon the snake was writhing about merrily, as healthy and fresh as if it had just been born.

Then, strangely, one day the snake bit the old woman. She screamed in agony as the poison sank into her bones.

As she lay dying, she cried out to the snake in anger and hurt, saying, "How could you have done this thing to me? I took you in, cared for you, nursed you back to health!"

To which the snake replied, "Look, you knew I was a snake. It's in my nature."

If you try to make a pet of an enemy, don't be surprised if you end up getting attacked in the end.

(Source: Traditional)

The Women at the Well

Once, two women set out with two wooden buckets to collect water at a nearby well. The women both started out with smiles, noting that it was an uncommonly bright, beautiful day.

The first woman dipped into the well and pulled out a bucket full of nice, clean water. She smiled happily and then said, "Here, let me get out of your way so that you may pull up a bucket of water for yourself."

So the second woman dipped into the well. However, when she brought up her bucket of water, it was filled with small rodents, dead birds, stones, and slimy things. It was undrinkable!

The woman wailed, "Oh why! How is it that you have pulled up a bucket of nice, clean drinking water, yet, when I dipped my bucket into the very same well, I pulled up nothing but froth and scum?"

But the first woman had long gone, leaving the second woman to weep and moan while the wind blew across the lonely plain.

*Sometimes there is no helping the twists
and turns of fate.*

(Source: Unknown)

The Seer

A famous seer sat in the marketplace telling fortunes as people passed by. He was making quite a bit of money, and his strange table was littered high with golden coins.

Suddenly, a man came running up to him. The man's face was flushed with excitement as he told the Seer, "Sir! I regret to tell you that your house has been broken into, and a thief is running off with all of your things!"

The Seer shrieked in outrage, and, getting up from his table (careful to brush all of the gold coins into his purse first), he hurried off through the crowded market in the direction of his house.

At this, all of the people laughed. One exclaimed, "How is it he could tell the future of so many strangers, but was blind as to his own future?"

Sometimes, people can see the trouble others are in danger of becoming entangled in better than than they can see their own!

(Source: Aesop)

The Graven Image

Once, in a dark land where men still prayed before ancient idols, there was a villager with a household god made of wood.

Often, he showed devotion to this god, but he was sorely vexed; it had never granted him a single request, and he lived in abject poverty.

Finally, his father advised him to rid himself of the useless idol, and worship a god that at least had his best interests at heart. Thus, in a fit of rage, the villager smashed the wooden image to bits.

Gold coins, which had been hidden in the wood long ago, came flying out of the splintered remains!

Sometimes our greatest treasure is hidden right under our noses!

(Source: Aesop)

The Boy's Toe Bone

Once there was a young boy sitting and playing a reed pipe on the banks of the Ganges. He was tending a flock of sheep. Soon, he was approached by an hungry lion, who considering him said, "You must now choose, my son: Shall I eat your sheep, or shall I eat you? For, as much as I love a sheep, I love the taste of human flesh so much more."

To which the young boy replied, "Oh sir! I will have to go and ask my mother, for these are her sheep. And, of course, I do not desire that you should eat me."

So the boy went to his mother and said, "Mother, today a hungry lion approached me as I was playing my reed pipe down by the river. He gave me a choice as to whether or not he should eat the sheep or eat me. What should I tell him?"

And the mother's eyes bulged with anger, and having a disgusted look on her face, she said, "Why, you should let him eat YOU of course!"

And so the boy went back to the banks of the river, and played his reed pipe, and the next day, while he was tending the sheep, the lion approached again, and said, "You are such a polite boy, it seems a shame I shall probably have to eat you if I cannot eat your sheep. Tell me: What did your mother tell you to do?"

And the boy answered, "Sir! My mother said you should most certainly eat me and leave the sheep alone."

And so the lion approached the boy with his slavering jaws held open. But, before he could pounce, the boy held up his hands and said, "One thing first, if you please! I ask only that you leave my bones at the foot of this tree, but the bone of my little toe, I wish you tie up in a knot in one of the branches, so it will swing in the wind."

And so the lion devoured the boy, but was careful to leave the pile of his bones at the foot of the tree, as per his request. The second request was trickier (after all, whoever heard of a lion climbing a tree?), but the great King of the Jungle managed to tie the toe bone in a knot on one of the branches, so that it swung back and forth in the wind. Then he departed to find new quarry.

It was not long before a group of robbers came and, seeing the flock of sheep left unattended, decided they must steal them. Just then, though, the leader of the robbers heard a click-clacking in the branches above him. He said, "Hark! I think I hear a ghost in the trees."

The other robbers, a superstitious bunch, looked about nervously. Then, the little toe bone fell from its place swinging from the branch, and smacked the leader of the robbers square on his head. The man gave out a great cry, thinking that the sky was falling!

"We are being attacked because of our great evil! Let us flee!"

And so the robbers ran away. The little toe bone fell on top of the pile of bones at the foot of the tree. It transformed itself back into a whole boy again, who sat by the banks of the river, tending his sheep and playing his pipes.

Don't let your fears and worries turn you away from your goal.

(Source: Hindu folktale)

The Priest and the Robber!

Once, in the long ago, a timid priest was making his way down a deserted forest lane. He was soon waylaid by a robber, who had been hiding in the bushes watching him with steely eyes.

The priest, a terrific fighter, soon grappled with the stranger, divesting him of his sword and throwing him to the ground. The priest picked up the sword, aimed it at the robber, and prepared to do him in.

Suddenly, the doomed bandit cried out, "Mercy! Oh, mercy upon me! How is it that you, who is committed to peace, can slay a man so easily in cold blood?"

The priest (who might be forgiven for recognizing that, indeed, it was anything but "in cold blood") stated plainly, "I slay thee not to destroy the peace, but to ensure it ever afterward!"

And with that, he ran the bandit through.

It is always better to fight and conquer evil than to submit and be its willing victim.

(Source: Turkey)

The Jackass and the Cur

Once upon a time, at Benares, there was an old washerman, who kept in his courtyard an ass that was tethered to a spit, and a mangy old dog that had free run of the place. The washerman lived as well as can be expected for a washerman and accumulated many fine possessions. He thought that, because of his loyal guard dog, his possessions were reasonably safe from burglars.

One day, he went to visit friends and left his animals in the courtyard to stand guard. As he left, a few burglars came creeping out of the bushes and began to carry away the possessions of the old washerman.

The jackass, seeing what was happening but unable to do anything to stop it, said to the dog, "You're a fine one! Why don't you bark or run after them, and try to stop them from robbing our master blind?"

To which the dog replied, "Well, it will teach him a lesson! He has become so accustomed to my guarding his house that he has begun to be neglectful of me! I have missed many meals now, as I'm sure you can see by my bony rib cage and lean shanks. So let them do what they will, I'll not raise a peep."

At this, the jackass was outraged, "How dare you demand pay when there is work to be done! You're a mean-spirited beast!"

And the dog replied, "And you truly are an ass! What sort of master would begrudge a servant his pay after the work is done?"

"Well," retorted the jackass, "I am going to do *my* duty, at any rate!" And with that, the Jackass let out such a bleating bray he frightened the robbers away. They took off running, just as the master came running back home.

Of course, the jackass was powerless to tell the master what had been occurring, and, since the robbers had left their booty behind in their panic, there was no evidence there had ever been any sort of crime occurring against the master at all.

The master was so enraged by the noisy commotion of the Jackass that he beat him mercilessly with a stick.

"No good deed ever goes unpunished."
Or, "Sometimes it is better just to stay quiet and
be thought a fool,
than open your mouth and remove all doubts."
Or something along those lines.

(Source: Hindu folktale)

13

The Story of Swing-Ear

Once, in the little village of Brahmaputra, a thief stole a valuable bell before running off into the jungle. Unluckily for him, however, he was quickly killed and devoured by a hungry tiger. His bell fell to the ground where the monkeys, finding its loud, resounding gongs amusing, spent their days playing with it.

Well, the other villagers found the scattered bones of the thief, and heard the sinister sounds of the strange bell (made by the monkeys swinging it), and soon a rumor crept through the town that there was a devilish monster lurking at the edge of town, a monster that captured men and devoured them whole, and who made a sound like a swinging bell wherever it went. In time, this legendary monster came to be known as "Swing-Ear."

The Rajah (ruler) of Brahamaputra was concerned about all of this, of course, but he did not know what to do. Soon, however, a wise old woman came to him and said, "Sire, if you allow me, I can soon settle this fiend, Swing-Ear."

He gave her leave to do so. So the old woman took a basket full of fruit and headed into the hills, where, soon, she spied the mischievous monkeys and their swinging bell. She scattered the fruit all over the ground and hid in the bushes.

Soon, the monkeys had completely forgotten their bell, and were busily picking the fruit off of the ground to eat. The bell lay on the ground, unattended. The wise old woman quickly scooped the thing up and ran away with it.

When the old woman returned, the people realized that they could no longer hear "Swing-Ear," and they thanked the old woman mightily. She became most honored and revered among the other villagers.

A little courage can win you much regard.

(Source: Hindu folktale)

14

Slow and Steady!

Once upon a time there was a slow, ambling, grumbling old tortoise. He went everywhere so slowly he could, at times, hardly be seen to be moving at all. Some passing him even thought him to have died!

His companion was a lightning-quick young hare, who was so fast he, at times, seemed to be a blur when he ran by. (All the better, after all, to make his escape from hunters and predators.)

Well, one day, the animals of the forest were congregating and making merry when one suggested they have a sort of contest. The wily fox came up with the idea that the hare should be pitted against the slow, meandering tortoise. All of the animals thought this to be the absolute height of humor, but the tortoise replied, "I bet I could beat the old thing, if I but tried! After all *slow and steady wins the race.*"

The hare thought this was too funny, and agreed readily to the race. He said, "That slow old thing? I could run circles around him in the time it takes for him to even get started!"

So the tortoise and the hare stood side by side, and the other animals gathered to watch. Suddenly, a squirrel dropped an acorn on a rock to announce the start of the race, and the hare took off like a streak of lightning. The tortoise, on the other hand, could barely move a few steps in the time it took the hare to be halfway finished with the race.

The hare looked back at the starting line, and, seeing that the tortoise had just barely started, laughed at himself and said, "I think I'll just lie down and take a little nap. I'll get some good rest, wake up, and make it to the finish line, and that slow old thing will still just barely be getting started!"

And so that is what he did. He fell fast asleep, dreaming little rabbit dreams.

Meanwhile, as the hare was fast asleep, the tortoise kept trudging on and on, finally making it to the halfway point in the race. The other animals were astounded at this, but the careful tortoise just kept huffing and puffing along, saying to himself, "Slow and steady wins the race! Slow and steady wins the race! Slow and steady wins!"

Sure enough, finally the tortoise made it a few steps from the finish line, and was just about to cross over when the arrogant hare awoke to see what a miserable blunder he had made. He tried to cross the distance between himself and the finish line, but, alas, he was too late. Due to his own arrogance and the persistence and determination of the tortoise, the hare actually *lost* what, to him, should have been an easy victory.

So the moral of this story is: slow and steady determination and effort will win over an arrogant, over-confident attitude.

Or, maybe it's that just because you seem over-qualified, you shouldn't be caught napping on the job, because that other fellow might just creep up on you and seize what should have been yours.

Or? Well, what do you think the moral of this story is?

(Source: Aesop)

Stone Soup

Once upon a time, a strange traveler entered a land where there had been a famine only a short time before. He went door to door, enquiring if he might purchase a little food from someone who might have stored some, but he was turned down again and again, with the door slammed in his face.

Finally, he took an iron pot and, setting it down at the side of the main road through the village, filled it with water from a nearby well and set it to boil. After doing this, he carefully placed a single large stone in the middle of the pot, making sure that some of the curious onlookers saw him do this.

"What on earth are you making?" inquired one curious woman as she approached the weary, hungry stranger.

The man, whose appearance was quite different from anything the villagers had hitherto seen, looked up and smiled, saying, "Stone soup, m'lady. I'm making stone soup."

And with that, he dipped in a large wooden spoon and tasted the broth. He said, "Not quite done yet. And, could use a little something . . . extra."

At this the woman found herself perplexed, asking, "But what do you mean it could use something extra?" She then got a knowing look on her face, snapped her fingers, and said, "I have just the thing! A few carrots I have had hidden away to eat if the food shortages should return. I'll tell you what: just let me go get them!"

And she ran back to her cottage, and came back with a sackful of carrots. The stranger smiled at her with gratitude, and tossed in the carrots. Well, after seeing this, another man came by and likewise asked what the two were doing.

"Making soup, m'lord! Stone soup . . . with a few carrots. But I tell you: I think the soup *still* needs something more."

The man beamed, said, "I know just what you mean! No soup is complete without a few potatoes. Why, I've had a few potatoes hidden away, just in case my family should go hungry. Why, I'll go get a few!"

And with that, a third onlooker came forward, and asked also what sort of broth they were bubbling. Being given the same answer as before, this villager went to fetch a few onions.

Still more came, some with a few cuts of beef, some with spices, some with a radish or some tomatoes. Finally, the pot of "stone soup" was bubbling with a delicious pot full of real soup, made from the hoarded food of the villagers.

"Best darn stone soup I ever tasted!" quoth the strange foreigner, who tasted the stuff but ate none of it himself. The villagers, meanwhile, gathered to pass around bowls full of the piping hot stuff, and enjoyed the best meal their community had ever had together.

The strange man had taught them all a lesson about the value of cooperation. As to what happened to him and where he went after the meal, the villagers searched to offer him a note of thanks. However, he had vanished . . . without a trace.

A little cooperation can save the day!

(Source: Traditional European folktale)

The Old Man and Death

There once was an old man sorely beset by many toils and much work. One day, when his withered old back was breaking under the weight of a heavy load of firewood, he cursed his sorry fate and exclaimed, "Oh! Would that DEATH could come and relieve a poor old man of these tiresome, trivial burdens."

Suddenly, out of the mist, a strange, horrible figure, a skeleton with bits and hunks of flesh still clinging to the bone, appeared. It pointed a long, bony finger at the old man and exclaimed, "What didst thou summon me for?"

The old man, so shortly before certain that he wanted to die, was suddenly seized by a fit of trembles. Shaking, he managed to stutter out, "O-o-oh! I simply wanted to know if thou couldst help an old man carry this burden of sticks home to his door! My back is fair killing me and about to give out!"

And that is how the old man lied to Death. And, did Death believe him? The story does not say.

Be careful what you wish for, as it might come true!

(Source: Aesop)

The Tortoise and the Eagle

Once upon a time, a slow, clumsy tortoise, who was forever going about back and forth with his head thrust into the dirt, met a noble eagle. The eagle, perched atop a nearby rock, was taking a break from his daily routine of flying the blue vault of the heavens and called down to the tortoise to be friendly.

"Hallo down there," he said. "How does it feel to be forever chained to the earth, while I am able to soar through the blue skies and be truly free?"

The eagle, though he did not mean it, must have sounded mighty arrogant to the lowly tortoise, who, at any rate, puffed out his chest (as best he was able) and said, "If you took me flying with you, it would be no time before I, too, had mastered the art, and could soar out on the winds as free as the breeze!"

The eagle, seeing that the tortoise thought quite a lot of his abilities, and that he was also quite mad, offered to let him try the impossible.

"Very well then. Come, I shall take you in my claws, and together we will soar higher than any tortoise, such as yourself, has ever soared before!"

And with that, the eagle scooped up the tortoise and soared high into the air, giving the tortoise the thrill-ride of his life. They went over mountain, and over forest, and over river, and over sea, but finally, coming to some jagged precipice, the Eagle said, "Now, my overconfident little friend, it is time you learned to fly on your own. Off you go!"

And with that, the eagle let go his hold upon the tortoise, and the little fellow went plummeting toward the jagged rocks. Try as he might, the tortoise found he simply could not fly.

He was dashed against the rocks. Later, the eagle flew back around, and seeing the lifeless remains of the tortoise in his broken shell, scooped up the parts he found succulent and good to eat.

And the moral is: Never let pride cloud your judgment.

(Source: Aesop)

Belling the Cat!

Once, when all the mice had gathered together, they had a council concerning what they were to do about the problem of the cat—for the cat was very sneaky and tricky and would often creep up on the mice when they were unsuspecting and gobble them up whole.

One bright young fellow suddenly got an idea of what it was they should do.

"We shall attach a brass bell to the cat's neck, so that when he is creeping around to strike at us, the bell will swing and chime and will alert us to his presence, so that we can run away!"

The other mice agreed that, indeed, this was the best plan that they had heard so far and that it should be put into action as soon as possible. Then, one very wise old mouse suddenly piped up, asking, "And, which one of you, pray tell, is going to be the one to hang the bell around the cat's neck?"

The best laid plans of mice and men...

(Source: French Fable)

The Moose and the Catfish

Once, in the deep wilderness, an old moose was walking by a pond when he spied the catfish. The moose said, "You are so small and insignificant compared to me, I think I will simply crush you to teach you a lesson."

At this, the catfish was horrified. The moose bent down, holding his great horns down to gore the catfish where it cowered in the water. Unfortunately for the moose, he managed to gore himself with his own horns!

His hoof flared up into pain! The catfish, seeing his opportunity to escape, quickly swam away. The moose fell into the water, then, dragging himself out again , went into the forest. He was suffering great pain from goring himself, and presently he fell over and died.

It is immoral to despise someone just because they are smaller and weaker.

(Source: Native American folktale)

20

Death's Messengers

Once, long ago, when Death was walking down a lonely country road, he was met by a giant who said to him, "What, shall I step out of the way for one I could crush like a little insect between my thumb and forefinger?"

The giant then beat Death mercilessly, until he was bleeding upon the dusty carpet of earth. Soon, a kind traveler came by, and, seeing that Death was injured badly, took him, tended his wounds, and nursed him back to health.

Death soon recovered, but he said to the man, "Dost thou not realize who I am? Man, I am Death, and now I must take thee with me as I go."

But the traveler said, "What? Is this how thou wilt repay my great kindness to thee? By killing me?"

At this, Death became very remorseful, and said, "Well, because thou hast made such a sacrifice to aid me in my time of trouble, I shall not take thee now. And, when finally I do come for thee, I will send thee messengers to alert thee as to my coming."

And with that Death departed, and the man saw him no more.

Well, the man went about his business, and was sometimes ill, and sometimes injured, but, always he recovered to full health and enjoyed a long and prosperous life.

Finally, when he was a bent and stooped old man that had outlived all of his friends and family to a great old age, he was walking down his garden path when, suddenly, he turned and there before him stood Death!

"Prepare thyself. I have come for thee!"

At this the old man was very wroth, and said, "What about our bargain? Wouldst thou takest me having sent no messenger to warn me, as thou hast promised?"

At this, Death was indignant.

"Silence! Hast not thou heeded thy failing eyesight, the gout in thy limbs, thy toothache, and dizziness? I tell thee: all of these are Death's messengers. Likewise, did not my little brother Sleep come to thee every night, and didst thou not lie, night after night in slumber, as if thou wert already dead?"

At this, the man could make no answer, so he relented, and went with Death to the land from whence once borne, no traveler ever returns.

Death is nothing to fear, as we are aging and moving closer to it with every passing year.

(Source: The Brothers Grimm)

21

The Country Mouse and the City Mouse

Once, a poor country mouse with nought to eat but a few scraps of mouldy cheese was invited by his better-off city cousin to a feast at the home in which he dwelt.

Their family dinner having already ended, the dishes, still half filled with lukewarm food, were left to draw flies (and mice) upon the table. The two mice crept upon the table top and went to work, zealously eating their nibbling little fill. Just then, a raucous chorus of people broke through the dining room door. They sat themselves down at the dining room table, and began to eat the leftovers. It was the servants, who were generously given the leavings of the sumptuous dinner after the family was finished.

The two mice fled from the table in terror, as they recognized that the loud, rough servants would capture and kill them if they saw them. Later, the country mouse thanked his city cousin, but declined the offer to stay, preferring the relative safety of his old home to the hurly-burly and danger of city life, good food or no.

Sometimes it is better to be content
with what you have.

(Source: Aesop)

22

The Jackass and the Pigs

Once, there was a miserable, grumbling jackass, who was filled with envy when he saw how the pigs on his farm were treated. It seemed they were slopped with delectable vittles and then left to lie around all day and sleep. The Jackass wished for himself a comparable life, and so he said to himself, "I shall deceive my master and feign sickness, so as to get a nice and easy life like the pigs."

And so this he did, lying down in the stable and refusing to get up, and moaning and groaning as if in pain. The farmer at first tried to rouse him with the whip, but, seeing as this was no good, he said to his wife, "Apparently, our jackass is sick. We'll have to try and nurse him back to health."

And so the farmer gave him a pail of milk and a bucket of oats and let him lie there all day and do nothing. Soon, the Jackass, who was getting mightily hungry, began to chomp and eat the oats and then, having satisfied his hunger, lay back on the quiet earth and slept.

Soon, he peeped his eyes open at the arrival of a few men who were butchers. He saw them line the pigs up, one after another, and then, horrors! He saw the pigs slaughtered cruelly, gutted, and cut-up into pieces for market. The Jackass, who had grown quite fat recently, found himself terrified that they would soon slaughter him! For, wasn't he now living like the pigs?

So he immediately quit his playacting, and, bounding up from the ground, began to trot around briskly, as if he were the very picture of health. And so the farmer whipped him soundly and sent him back to work.

And the moral of the story is: Sometimes, the grass really is greener on the other side. Or, sometimes appearances can be deceiving. Or, sometimes it is better to be content with what we have, than covet what our neighbor has, as his circumstances may be completely different from our own.

(Source: Aesop)

The Farmer, the Fox, and the Hen

Once upon a time a conniving old fox crept into a chicken coop, snatching for himself as many of the plump chickens and eggs as he could swallow before making off like a bandit with the farmer being none the wiser.

This greatly upset the hen, who went to farmer and said, "*Cluck!* That terrible fox has been in the chicken coop! *Cluck!* You must do something to protect us! *Cluck!* If you don't act now, you'll lose all your chickens! *Cluck! Cluck!*"

And so the farmer, knowing that this was true, lie in wait one lonely, moonlit night, and watched and listened for the approach of the fox. Soon, he heard the old thing creeping through the brush, and he got out his heavy spade.

When the Fox tried to enter the door of the chicken coop, the farmer suddenly sprang upon him, yelling, "I'll teach you to steal my chickens, you dirty, sneaky varmint!" And with that, he beat the fox in the head until his eyes popped out and his brains were leaking out of his ears.

After the fox was dead, the old hen came waddling out of the chicken coop, and thanked the farmer for killing the fox. The farmer, who had forgotten to eat dinner, suddenly found he had worked up an appetite. He looked at the plump little hen, and his jaws began to drip, and his eyes bulged and his stomach rumbled. Suddenly, he reached down and grabbed the Hen by the neck.

He wrung the Hen's neck with his powerful hands; then, putting the carcass in a sack, he strode off for home, eager to clean and fry the bird and have a late-night snack.

The enemy of your enemy is not always your friend.

(Source: Aesop)

The Brahman and the Three Rogues

Once, there was a brahman who traveled to find a goat to sacrifice. Coming home along a forest path, he was met by three rogues, all of who wanted to divest him of the burden he was carrying over his shoulders.

Conceiving a plan, the first rogue said, "Brahman, why are you carrying that dead dog on your shoulders?"

At this the Brahman found himself sorely perplexed. He flung the goat from his shoulders and looked at it carefully. Then, shrugging at the first man's ignorance, he put the carcass back on his shoulders and continued onward.

The second rogue then called out, "Brahman, why are you carrying that dead dog on your shoulders?"

The Brahman, at hearing this, was once again confused and troubled. He whipped the dead animal off of his shoulders and examined it carefully. He then shrugged uneasily at the ignorance of the second man, and put the dead goat back on his shoulders, continuing (more nervously now) upon his way.

Finally, the third rogue called out from the path, "Brahman, why are you carrying that dead dog on your shoulders?"

At this, the Brahman finally lost his nerve, and, whipping the dead goat from his shoulders, he went and ran to the creek, carefully washing himself from what he was now convinced was the filthy contamination of carrying an unclean beast on his shoulders.

The rogues, having convinced the Brahman that a dead goat was, in fact, a dead dog, took the goat and cooked it, enjoying a hearty meal and laughing at their grand deception.

Sometimes, it is better to trust our own senses rather than listen to the carping opinions of others.

(Source: Hindu folklore)

25

The Fox and the Mask

Once, the nimble fox, who is ever lurking about looking for a free meal, crept into the home of a famous actor. The actor was away on business, but the fox managed to steal into his private wardrobe and find a beautiful, colored mask.

The fox, having never before seen such a thing, wondered at it, but was pleasantly amused to turn it around and see that the back of it was simply an empty space.

"Tis a pity!" exclaimed the fox. "Such a beautiful exterior, but wanting for a brain!"

Truly, a beautiful face is no substitute for intelligence.

(Source: Phaedrus)

26

The Miller, His Son, and Their Jackass

Once, coming from a long stay in a nearby village, a miller and his son led their slow, ponderous jackass through a dense wood. Soon, while plunging along the path, they came to a trio of girls, who began to point and laugh, saying, "Look at those fools, struggling along in the heat when they could be riding upon that jackass. At the very least, the miserable old man might let his little son climb on the back of the jackass and rest!"

The miller, not wishing to be mocked, commanded his son to ride upon the back of the jackass, and the son soon climbed on back of the creature. It was not long, however, before the man and his son met up with a trio of old codgers, who pointed with scorn at the lad riding the jackass, saying, "Look at how the young treat the old these days! Why, that healthy young scoundrel is riding that jackass and forcing his poor old father to walk along in this heat! It's disgraceful!"

The miller, not wanting to be spoken of in these harsh terms, commanded his little son to dismount from the jackass and got on the animal's back himself. They proceeded on their way, but soon came to a trio of young boys, one of whom pointed in mockery and derision, and said, "Look at that selfish old man riding that jackass! He is making his young son walk along in this heat! Why, shouldn't they really be riding the jackass together?"

At this, the miller again found himself sorely perplexed. So he hopped up on the jackass along with his son, and the two continued to ride.

Soon, however, they came to an animal husbandman, who, seeing both the miller and his son sitting astride the struggling jackass, yelled out in consternation, "Look at those lazy fools! They have loaded that poor jackass down to the point where it can barely creep along in this abominable heat. Such as them should be taken and horsewhipped for their cruelty to dumb animals!"

At hearing this, the miller yet again found himself facing the opprobrium of a complete stranger. So, thinking quickly, he commanded his son to get off the jackass, and he set about carefully binding the animal's hooves. Then, by aid of a stout tree limb, he and his son hoisted the jackass between them, and carried him along on their shoulders. (Which, truth be told, was quite a sight to see.)

A band of traveling pilgrims spied them, however, and found themselves too dumbfounded to make any utterance. Just as the shocked pilgrims came upon the scene, the braying, struggling jackass kicked free of its bonds, and, giving the idiot miller and his son a series of punishing kicks, ran of into the brush, never to be seen again.

The group of pilgrims began to laugh and point, in spite of themselves, and the miller and his son were forced to walk home in humiliation. The strange fiasco of the miller and his son carrying their jackass between them was talked about in town for years thereafter.

So the miller lost both his dignity *and* his jackass.

By trying to please everyone, you never really please anyone. Please yourself.

(Source: Phaedrus)

27

The Simpleton's Jackass

Once, two rogues spotted a simpleton leading a jackass by a leash. One rogue said to the other, "Watch, I'll rob that fool of his jackass just as easily as anything you've ever seen!"

And so the two rogues walked behind the simpleton, and, sneaking the leash from the jackass' neck, he put it on his own while his comrade led the mule away.

When the simpleton turned around and spied what he still thought to be his jackass, he was utterly astounded to see a man standing there in its place.

"Who in the world are you?" cried the simpleton in amazement. The thief replied, "I am your poor jackass, except I am really a man! Once, long ago, when I came home drunk, as I did very often in those days, my mother called down the curse of Allah upon my head. I soon found myself transformed into a jackass and have walked the earth in this unfortunate guise ever since. My mother must have prayed for mercy for me, for I have transformed back into a human while you have been leading me home."

At this, the simpleton was most aggrieved, and exclaimed, "Oh! You poor, unfortunate man! I'll free you at once!"

And so the thief took off his lead and ran away to join his friend and the jackass they had stolen. The simpleton went back to his wife, who inquired angrily after the lost jackass.

The simpleton replied, "Oh, my wife! We have made a terrible mistake, for our jackass was really a man. Allah transformed him into the shape of a jackass to punish him, but now he has changed back, and I have let him go!"

At this the wife was sore afraid, as she feared the judgment of Allah for all the bad treatment they had meted out to the jackass. Both of them hid in their home for many days, scarcely daring to venture out in their gloom and despair.

Finally, hungry and lacking money, the wife commanded that the simpleton go out and buy another jackass, so as to do a little honest labor and earn some bread. The simpleton went to the village to do just this.

The thieves, in the meantime, had sold the simpleton's jackass to the man who dealt in livestock, and it was here that the simpleton went in search of another animal to buy.

How amazed he must have been when, among the herd, he found what was, unmistakably, his old jackass! After confirming this to his own personal satisfaction, the simpleton became quite indignant, and, shaking his finger at the beast, he exclaimed, "You sinful, disgraceful man you! You must have gone home drunk yet again!"

Once a fool, always a fool.

(Source: *Arabian Nights*)

28

The Ox and the Frog

Once, in the long ago times, a simple family of frogs were disporting themselves in a muddy creek when a giant ox came blundering along. The magnificent, humongous animal stepped on half-a-dozen frogs, crushing them into pulp. One of the frogs who managed to escape went back to his mother, who was quite a puffed-up and proud specimen of her kind.

"Oh, Mother!" the frog exclaimed. "A tremendous large creature came blundering along and killed half of our family! I have never seen such a gigantic creature before, and pray I never see one again!"

Distressed at this, the frog's mother said, "Well, how big of a creature was it? Was it this big?"

And the frog-mother puffed out her cheeks until she was twice her normal size.

At this, the little frog said, "Oh no, Mother; it was far, far bigger than that! Why, a person could scarce imagine a creature so enormous!"

At this, the proud frog-mother grew indignant and said, "Well, how about this? Was the beast this big?"

And she blew herself up to an even more enormous size with her green, spotted cheeks bulging like twin balloons. Her son merely croaked with laughter, and said, "Oh no, Mother! If you blew and blew until you were twenty times that size, you would still not equal one half the size of this great monster!"

But the frog-mother, not really listening to what her son had to say, said (albeit with some difficulty): "WELL, HOW ABOUT NOW? WAS HE THIS SIZE?"

And she blew until she was quite enormous.

Suddenly, there was a tremendous . . . *POP!*

Greasy, gooey innards flew fast and furiously into the face of the frightened frog. His mother, in all her indignant pride, had managed to pop her own head open!

"Hmmm," said a passing toad. "That will teach the old thing to always be so puffed-up!"

It never pays to mimic a glory that is not rightfully ours.

Source: French Fable

The Bittern and the Mussel

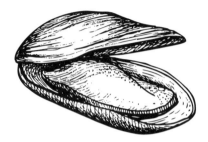

Once, upon the rocky coast, a mussel was basking in the warm sunshine when a bittern came along, and plunging its beak inside, attempted to eat the mussel's soft flesh.

In reaction to this, the mussel snapped shut its shell, and the bittern's beak became caught. At a sort of stand-off, the bittern said to the mussel, "If you don't open your shell today, if you don't open your shell tomorrow, there will be a dead mussel."

At this, the mussel grew defiant.

"Dear bittern," it said, "if you don't take out your beak today, if you don't take out your beak tomorrow, there will be a dead bittern."

Neither creature willing to yield to the other, both of them froze in their respective positions until a hungry fisherman came along, snatched up both of them, and took them both home to eat.

Sometimes, you must learn to compromise with an enemy, or you will both be destroyed.

(Source: Chinese fable)

The Eagle and the Spider

Once, the mighty Eagle soared upward to the edge of a tall peak and, looking down, surveyed his mighty kingdom with a proud, arrogant eye.

"I am the mightiest creature in all the forest. For, in truth, none can fly so high and so far as myself."

Just then, the spider, who was spinning a web in the tree that grew upon the mountain above, said, "You boastful old thing! Look how high I have ascended, and I have neither feather or wing to propel me!"

At this, the proud Eagle was exceedingly perplexed, and said, "How did you manage to get up so high, yet, you obviously cannot fly?"

To which the Spider responded, "By crawling upon your back and holding onto your tail feathers, you silly thing! Now look at me! I am truly the loftiest creature in all of existence!"

Just then, a mighty wind picked up and swept the Spider and his fancy web from the branches of the leaning tree, into the vast gulf below.

Pride goeth before a fall, as the Good Book says.

(Source: Russian fable)

The Wolf and the Fox

A young Wolf was rhapsodizing on the greatness of his father, who had recently passed.

"How proud I am to bask in the glory of my father's legacy. For, did he not teach the entire neighborhood to tremble with fear at him? He, who easily bested 200 enemies in his day, sending their chastised souls to the kingdom of death!"

At this, the Fox thought for awhile and decided that, verily, what the Wolf said did not, entirely, ring true. So he responded, "Yes, you do, indeed, seem to have reason to be so boastful and proud. Yet, I wonder: should you not stop to consider that your father's '200' victims were almost entirely made up of sheep and asses? And that, the one time *he lost* a battle was the only time he ever sparred with an angry Ox; the result of which lea to the reason you are mourning him now?"

Before you exalt in the greatness of another, make sure their reputation is well-deserved.

(Source: German fable)

Slow-Coil and King Frog

Once, there lived an old serpent named Slow-Coil, who was so old and tired he could no longer catch food for himself. Alas, he lay upon the edge of the creek all day, waiting to die.

Soon, happened along a little frog who, seeing the pitiful serpent, asked him what was the matter.

At this, Slow-Coil hissed, "Oh! Because I bit and killed the son of a powerful Brahman named Kaundinya, when I was slithering around Brahmapootra, he cursed me to carry frogs upon my back all of the day. So here I lie, waiting for a chance to carry a little frog upon my back. Would you like to be the first?"

And, though the little frog didn't dare to crawl upon Slow-Coil's back, he decided to go and tell his king all that he had heard. The frog king came back to visit Slow-Coil, and asked him if what he said was true.

"Oh yes! I am doomed to carry frogs upon my back! Here, climb aboard, and I will carry you across this stream."

And so the frog king did just that. And, having liked the trip so much by the time it was over, he began to use Slow-Coil to ferry him across the water all the time. He felt secure that the old serpent would never put the bite on him. After all: Hadn't Kaundinya cursed him to carry frogs?

Well, not long after, the frog king crawled upon the serpent's back, but, instead of slithering down into the water, his head shot around and he complained bitterly to the frog about how hungry he was.

The frog king considered.

"Well, go ahead and eat some of my frogs. I give you leave to do so."

And so Slow-Coil began to gulp down the frogs. And the very last frog he ate was the frog king himself.

Watch out for an enemy who seems eager,
all of a sudden, to do you many kind favors.
Chances are, they are after something they can get
easier by craft and guile than by brute force.

(Source: Hindu folklore)

The Jackass and the Horse

Once, in the long ago times, a jackass was loaded down by an inconsiderate, foolish master with a burden that was too much for him to bear. Trotting along beside him, as free and easy as the breeze, an ignoble old mare was happy to be carrying relatively little.

"Please, horse, take some of this burden I am carrying off of my back. For, though the master doesn't realize it, I am nearing exhaustion, and if I carry this heavy load much longer, I will surely die!"

The horse whinnied in reply, "Don't come to me with your petty complaints and trivial grumbles! I'm loved and respected enough not to be saddled with such a heavy burden!"

At this, the horse trotted on, leaving the poor jackass to struggle under his load. Soon, the poor animal did, indeed, drop dead.

The foolish master was very disturbed by this, but, being a fool, unhitched the heavy load the jackass was carrying, and put it on the horse's back, making him carry double. Then because the poor fool didn't have the heart just to leave the faithful old jackass in the forest for any wolf or bear to happen along and devour, he took the carcass of the animal, and threw *that* over the Horse's back as well! (We suppose he intended to take it home and bury it on his farm.)

Now the horse found that, because he had refused to help the jackass, and the jackass had died, he was now taxed with carrying not only his own burden, but the huge burden of the jackass, and the jackass's dead body as well! An agonizing load of weight, even for a sturdy horse!

Sometimes, taking on a little extra trouble now can save one from much heartache and toil at a future time.

(Source: France)

34

The Jackal and the Elephant's Carcass

Once, when the Bodhisattva was reborn into this life, he came back as a wild jackal, driven by strange cravings.

Now, the Jackal was a greedy creature that went to and fro in the forest looking for prey. One day, as he was walking by the river, he came across the carcass of a dying elephant, that had dropped while taking water.

The Jackal quickly seized the opportunity, pouncing upon the still-warm carcass. However, he found that he could not, try as he might, chew through the tough trunk, which was like trying to chew through a huge serpent. Likewise, the tusks were like chomping down on bone.

The head and eyes appealed very little to him, and the feet were solid and too chewy to be enjoyable. There was too much belly for him to even contemplate where to begin, so the Jackal found himself in a quandary.

Of course, being what he was, he could just abandon the carcass to the other predators and go find some smaller, daintier morsel. But his greed got the better of him; he couldn't stand the thought of going and leaving all that meat behind. So he went around to the rear of the creature and ... aha!

He began to eat his way inside from the rear, chomping and munching all the tasty innards, and washing it down with thick, syrupy elephant blood. Then, like Jonah in the whale, he found himself in the belly of the beast, but was quite content to curl up and take a little nap while his food digested.

"I am quite comfortable and warm in here tonight," the Jackal said to himself, "so why should I leave?"

Unfortunately for the Jackal, though, a torrential rain came pouring down, and by the time he awoke, the blazing sun had shrunk the elephant skin until he found himself wrapped, like a bug in a cocoon, in tough hide. And the weather became sweltering!

He found he could barely breathe, and he began to panic from being so imprisoned. He struggled and struggled, but to no avail.

Finally, exhausted and gasping for air (and no doubt parched from thirst), the Jackal gave up, and quit struggling and resigned himself to a slow, terrible death.

Lucky for him, though, another monsoon swept through, loosening the taut, dried flesh until, awakening with a start, the crafty Jackal soon realized it would indeed be possible for him to escape.

He fought his way with a tremendous struggle, tearing bits of flesh as he went out the mouth of the elephant's carcass, and onto the muddy, dirty ground.

The heavy rain and fresh air never seemed so good to him. He quickly said to himself, "I have learned a significant lesson: I will never ever let greed get the best of me again, or cloud my judgment."

And he never did.

And the moral of the story is, "Greed can make prisoners of us all."

(Source: Indian folklore)

35

The Simpleton Breaks a Window

Once, a man entered his favorite store and, unthinkingly, managed to break a delicate glass object. Feeling terrible, he straightway confessed it to the proprietor, who, sweeping up the mess, patted the man on the shoulder and said, "Eh, what is it to me? You are my best customer. Come, let's have a drink together. I'll cover the cost."

And with that, he got his best bottle of schnapps and proceeded to drink with the customer who had broken the precious glass item.

Now, also in the store at the time, and overhearing this, was a simpleton, who was much given to drink and profligate living. He said to himself, considering, "Hmmm. That man broke an expensive glass item, and the store owner has treated him to a glass of schnapps. If I broke the store front window, I suppose I would be treated to an entire bottle of schnapps!"

And, to test out his hare-brained theory, he went outside, found the biggest loose paving stone he could find, and tossed it through the store window.

The huge glass pane shattered into a million pieces.

To the simpleton's surprise, the store owner came rushing out in a murderous rage, beating the simpleton with his fists until the vagrant lout begged him to cease.

"Why are you beating me? That other man broke an expensive glass toy, and you treated him to schnapps. Me, I broke a huge and expensive glass window, yet, you beat me!"

And to this, the store keeper replied, "Of course I beat you! That man is my best customer! If he breaks a small item, so what? What does it matter to me? But you? You broke a *huge* item, and you have never earned me a single nickel. Tell me: What have you ever done for me to be forgiven for committing such a stupid, pointless error?"

And so, this story was told by a rabbi to a young scholar, who had questioned the prophets, and invoked the opinions of Moses Ben Maimon to justify his heresy.

His rabbi reminded him of the greatness of Moses Ben Maimon, and told this story to illustrate that, while Moses Ben Maimon might be forgiven a small heresy because of his great devotion and contribution to the faith, the young Talmudic scholar had done *nothing* himself to justify or excuse his "breaking the shop window" of their religion.

So the moral of this story, perhaps, is: don't point out the wrongheaded ideas of great men to excuse the wrongheaded ideas of the petty. Or?

(Source: Jewish folklore)

36

The Peacock and the Crow

Once, all the animals of the forest got together to have a beauty contest. Among them were the crow and the peacock. Now, in those days, neither of these fine birds were very much to look at, so, knowing that in their present condition they could, neither one, hope to win the beauty contest, they devised a special plan.

"We will paint our feathers merry colors, and make ourselves more beautiful for the contest! Thus, one of us will be assured to win. Come, you shall paint me, and then I shall paint you."

And so the two birds both gathered pots of paint, and the crow took his time making the peacock as beautiful as he possibly could, painting him with a rainbow of bright, vibrant colors. Thus, the peacock became a most impressive sight to behold.

Then, the crow said, "You must paint me now!"

But the scheming peacock had another idea. "Come here, my little friend, and I will paint you as a bird has never been painted before."

And the crow went to the peacock and closed his eyes. The peacock began to paint; but, instead of using the full range of colors as the crow had done when painting him, he used only the color black. Thus, the peacock felt doubly certain that he, and only he, would win the beauty competition. And, of course, that is exactly what happened.

And the moral of this story is:
never leave your fate in the hands of another. Or, never let another do what you can do for yourself.

(Source: China)

56

Good for Evil

Once there was a wise man who was walking along, minding his own business and preoccupied with his deep, deep thoughts, when he happened upon a coiling python caught in a trap.

"It isn't right," he said to himself, "to leave the poor creature to die in pain. I will release it."

He promptly freed the serpent from the trap; but, to his surprise, it immediately proceeded to wind itself around his body, preparing to eat him!

"Wait!" cried the wise man in terror. "You can't repay good with evil!"

At this, the serpent considered.

"True," he said. "One should take care never to repay good for evil. But, I am hungry, so your logic falls on deaf ears." (Note: It can be demonstrated scientifically that snakes really are deaf.)

"Wait! Before you proceed, I suggest we gather the opinions of a few more knowledgable sources, so as to have all the information we can before the act is commenced."

And the serpent (who was altogether, one can see, a most reasonable fellow, despite the fact that he was a hungry predator) agreed to this readily.

Just then, a beaten-down old nag happened by.

"Mr. Horse," asked the wise man, "is it ever okay to repay good with evil?"

And the horse (who was a sort of sad, bitter fellow) said, "I don't suppose so. But, it *is* the custom around these parts. Take me for instance: I spent the best years of my life breaking my back for my master, just to be turned out when I was old and no longer of any use. Now, I am left to wander these woods until I die."

And with that, the tragic old mare trotted off and the serpent opened his wide jaws very wide and started to squeeze the wise man to death, so as to better be able to swallow him whole.

"Wait!" cried the wise man. "We have only had the opinion of one! Why, here comes the wise ox. He will know right from wrong!"

And so, the serpent was persuaded to stop eating the wise man, and the wise man then asked the ox, "Mr. Ox, is it ever okay to repay good with evil?"

And the ox lowered his horned head, and thought and then said, "No, probably not. But, it *is* the custom around these parts, I'm afraid."

And with that, the wise ox trotted off.

And the serpent, who, by this time was famished, proceeded once more to batten upon the living flesh of the wise man, when he cried out, "Wait! We have only asked a horse and an ox! Let's ask that young coyote over there what he thinks! Surely, his opinion is worth adding to the others."

So the serpent was again persuaded to stop his planned preying on the wise man for a moment so that he might ask the coyote if he thought it was ever okay to repay good with evil.

"Mr. Coyote..." began the wise man.

After listening carefully, the coyote asked the serpent, "Now, how was it you were trapped in the snare when he found you. Are you sure you were securely fastened, with no means of escape? It is important, since the whole question hinges on whether or not he actually saved your life, and thus, did you good, which you propose to repay with evil."

At the suggestion that the trap might have been a phoney, and the serpent merely conning to capture the wise man as prey, the serpent became indignant. He crawled back into the trap, and the coyote merely looked at him and said, "Yes, I guess everything is as good now as it was before I happened upon the scene."

And with that, the coyote and the wise man walked away.

Now the wise man said to the coyote, "I'll show you that it is right to repay good with good. Come to my farm every morning from now on, and I'll give you one hen and a bottle of sotol."

At this, the coyote readily agreed.

So every morning, the coyote came to the farm, while the wise man's dog was tied up, and got his free hen and his bottle of sotol. Soon, however, he became lazy, and began to demand more.

Now, one hen and one bottle of sotol was not enough for him, but he had to have double his ration.

"And you don't dare say no to me, wise man! I can come to your farm and cause plenty of trouble! Besides, you yourself said it was wrong to repay good with evil, and I have saved your life once already!"

Upon hearing this, the dog became disgusted and said, "Soon he will be demanding three times what he already gets. No, this cannot go on like this. Tomorrow, when you take him his sacks full of sotol and fresh hens, put me in one of them, and I'll deal with him in my own way."

And so, the wise man, not wishing to come to ruin either way, obeyed the very wise dog and put him in a sack like the liquor and the hens. When he went to meet the coyote the next day, he let first one, then another, hen out of the sacks.

The coyote quickly pounced on them, gobbled them up, and finished the meal with his bottles of liquor, Then, feeling stuffed and drunk and greedy, he wiped his dripping snout with his paw and said, "Well, what else have you got for me?"

The wise man then opened the third sack, and out jumped the angry, ferocious dog. The coyote, too drunk and stuffed to run away, tried to scramble to safety, but the dog was too swift for him. The dog bore down on the coyote with killing intensity, and, before he died, the coyote cried out to the wise man: "B-but what about your unwillingness to repay good with evil?"

To this the wise man merely laughed. "Oh si, Senor Coyote, but, you see, it *is* the custom around these parts!"

Sometimes, no matter how much good you intend to do, it just doesn't turn out the way you expect.

(Source: Mexican folktale)

The Last Laugh

Once, an infidel who scoffed at religion went to visit the oracle at Delphi. Here he conceived to trick Apollo by holding a sparrow in his pocket. He conceived to ask Apollo if the bird in his pocket was either dead or alive. For, he thought to himself, "If he sayeth it is dead, I can produce it alive as proof of his error. And if he sayeth it be alive, it is but the work of a moment to crush it. Either way, he shall be proved wrong."

So, approaching the Pythoness, the infidel asked the oracle of Apollo, "Is the bird in my pocket alive or dead?"

The Pythoness (whose mouth Apollo spoke through) laughed, saying, "It is both to thee, as thou couldst crush the life from it in a moment, or let the bird live, all the better to try and trick me. However, as to me and thee, thou art most surely as dead as thy spirit."

And with that, Apollo struck the life from the infidel.

He who laughs last, most assuredly laughs loudest. (Alternately: it is never a good idea to laugh at things sacred or holy. Or, pride goeth before a fall. Or, various other interpretations...)

(Source: Aesop)

The Sparrows and the Flax

Once, when all the sparrows were gathered for a council, one wise old bird told the younger ones, "Make sure and go to eat up all the seeds planted in that new field. For, they have planted flax, and when it grows, it will be spun into nets!"

But the younger sparrows merely laughed.

"What concern is that to us?" they asked. "We will simply fly away when the nets come out! Now, be still and go away, you silly old bird!"

At this, the old bird was wroth with the silly young ones and, as the seeds began to sprout told them, "Now you go and uproot those sprouts! For destruction has come upon us, and we shall fall victims to man's cleverness!"

But the young sparrows continued to laugh, and they scorned the old bird so that she flew away in anger, making her a nest in the rafters of an old barn.

The younger sparrows continued to fly in and out of the new field until, one day, the heavy nets, into which the flax was spun, were produced by eager farmhands, who wasted no time in capturing and killing the young birds.

Sometimes it is best to listen to the wisdom of our elders, even if it seems foolish and quaint.

(Source: Aesop)

The Ostrich, the Eagle, and the Reindeer

Once, the ungainly ostrich was spotted by the swift, lightning-like reindeer, who observed, "The ostrich cannot run very well, but it undoubtedly can fly very swift and far."

The reindeer didn't realize that the ostrich could not fly.

On another day, the fearless, noble eagle spotted the ostrich going about his business, and observed, "It is true that the poor ostrich cannot fly, but I suppose he runs as fleet and fast as any other animal."

Never judge a person by how they look on the outside.

(Source: German fable)

The Blind Man and the Snake

Once, two men were traveling together, and one of them was nearly blind. At one point in the journey, the blind man lifted his arm and managed to throw his whip away. Although he and his companion searched and searched, they could not find the whip.

Walking back to where the horses were hitched, the man came across a twisted knot of cord lying on the ground. Delighted, he thought he had found his lost whip, but soon realized he had not.

"At any rate," he said to himself, "I have found myself a nice new whip, and that is much better!"

What the blind man did not realize was that he had actually picked up a sleeping snake, mistaking it for a leather rope.

He put the snake in his pocket, mounted his horse, and drove off with his companion. When he pulled the snake from his pocket, his companion was aghast with horror.

"Throw that away! That is not a whip!" he spat. "You have mistakenly picked up a dangerous snake, you blind man!"

But the blind man became suspicious, telling him, "My friend, it is obvious you envy the excellent whip I have managed to find. Here, let us travel on to the next village, and there you can seek out a new whip for yourself, and God willing, you will find one of the same quality."

And his companion answered him, "Old fool, what I have told you is the truth! I do not desire to possess a deadly serpent. Now toss that thing away, before it kills you!"

And the blind man (who must have been cheated a great deal in his life to be so suspicious) retorted, "You just want me to throw away my nice new whip, so that you can go and fetch it later and have it for yourself! Well, I'll not do it, I tell you!"

At this, his companion saw that any further argument was fruitless. He sighed and rode away, leaving the blind man to his fate.

Soon, the serpent came back to full wakefulness, and, seizing upon his opportunities, wound himself around the blind man's throat, squeezing the life out him and devouring his carcass on the ground at his leisure.

Sometimes what is most dangerous to you is right in front of you, but you refuse to see it.

(Source: Persian folklore)

Brother Rat and Brother Toad

Once, long ago, Brother Rat laughed at his brother Toad, saying, "I can do more than you. I can run, and you can only hop. Therefore, I am the better one."

Brother Toad was sure, somehow, that Brother Rat was wrong about this, and so he said, "I'll tell you what: let's test this for the record. You see those men over there taking their lunch? Well, watch what happens when I hop over there and introduce myself to them!"

And with that, Brother Toad hopped on over to where the men were taking their lunch break. The men exclaimed, "Oh, how awful! There is a disgusting toad!"

However, the men continued to eat their lunches relatively undisturbed. Brother Rat looked at this, puzzled. Brother Toad hopped back, and then said, "Now, you try it. Run up to the men eating their lunches, and see what happens."

Brother Rat did just that. When he made himself known to the men, however, instead of just pointing at him and then ignoring him like they did Brother Toad, the men shouted, exclaimed, "Look! A disgusting rat! We must kill it!" and picked up sticks and stones to try and beat and crush him to death!

Brother Rat fled as fast as he could back to Brother Toad who laughing exclaimed, "I knew exactly what would happen, of course. Now, just you take a lesson at this. Not everyone who seems to be less advantaged actually is."

Also, we might add, the moral could possibly be that everyone has different and unique capabilities.

(Source: African fable)

43

Trishka's Caftan

Once, a peasant named Trishka saw that his caftan, or long coat, was getting threadbare at the elbows. "No difficulty there," he said to himself. "I'll simply cut the ends off the sleeves, and use them to patch the elbows. This he did with what he thought were outstanding results.

Unfortunately, not a one of his neighbors saw it the same way, as now, though the elbows were as good as new, the arms were quite short and comical-looking, causing people who saw him to snicker behind their hands.

Trishka was quite hurt by this, but decided, "I shall simply cut the material from the hem of my caftan, and use it to repair the sleeves. Oh, how clever I am when I put my mind to something!"

And so he cut the material from the end of the long, skirt-like coat, and lengthened his sleeves. Now, however, people laughed outright at him as he went down the street, as, even though the arms and sleeves of his caftan were right and proper, the traditionally ankle-length garment was now much shorter than any caftan should be.

And the moral of the story is:
Don't rob Peter to pay Paul.

(Source: Russian fable)

44

The Owls and the Crows

Once, there lived a family of owls next to a family of crows. Now, the owls did not care for the crows, and neither did the crows care for the owls. They were constantly scheming as to how to get the best of each other when, one day, a very wise old crow came to his fellows and said, "I have a plan to finally get rid of those awful owls. First though, you must fall upon me, and pluck a few of my feathers and poke and prod me as if you wanted to attack and kill me. Then, leave me for dead. I will do the rest."

And so the crows all fell upon their brother, and poked him, and plucked his feathers, and bloodied him, and battered him about, and left him for dead. And, soon, curious as to what was going on outside their own nest, the so-curious owls came flying over to examine the poor, battered crow.

"Oh, thank heavens!" exclaimed the crow. "My people have cast me out, and I have no where else to turn! Could you not find it in your hearts to allow a poor, beaten, defenseless crow such as myself to warm himself and heal in your nest? After all, I am no longer cared for by my own kind."

The owls all had a special meeting and decided that this would be a good thing to do. So they allowed the crow to move himself into their nest, and recuperate, and grow the feathers he had lost back, slowly but surely.

Soon, the icy winds of winter began to blow across the forest, and Mr. Crow could be seen gathering kindling around the nest of the owls. The owls asked him, "Mr. Crow, why are you doing that?"

To which he replied, "Eh? Oh, well, I am simply gathering wood to make a barrier between ourselves and the cold, cold wind."

Mr. Crow's feathers had healed well enough for him to take flight. As soon as he could do so, he went and stole a firebrand from some peasant's fireplace, and, returning to the nest of the owls, set fire to the wooden barrier he had himself erected.

The owls were smothered by the heavy black smoke, and all of them died.

And the moral of this story is:
NEVER TRUST A RENEGADE.

(Source: Chinese Fable)

The Foolish Monkeys

Once at Benares, the king had a beautiful garden that was the delight of all who entered it. In this garden lived a family of monkeys, who were likewise the delight of all who entered the garden but who were pests to the gardener.

One day, when the gardener was very busy, he thought to himself, "I'll finally get some use out of those pesky monkeys! I'll set them to perform a task even they cannot possibly foul up!"

And so the gardener, who was much too busy to water the trees (what on else would a gardener have to do? one wonders) went to the Monkey King and asked him politely if he and his family could be entrusted to the task.

"Oh, certainly!" said Papa Monkey, taking a bucket of water and passing it down to his wife and sons. "You can certainly rely on us!"

And so the gardener left them to their work. At first, all went smoothly, but then Papa Monkey had a bright idea.

"We must pull up all the trees!" he said. "And we must then examine the roots. For, trees with long roots need much water, while trees with short roots should need hardly any at all!"

And so the monkeys stopped their watering and pulled up all the trees to examine the roots.

So, of course, all the trees then died.

It is not good to trust ANYTHING to a pack of fools.

(Source: India)

A Clever Ape and a Foolish Wolf

Once, in the long ago times, a tricky, mischievous ape was making sport of the noble lion. He was imitating the lion's every move, as apes are wont to do, and the lion, looking up at the ape gamboling and chattering about in the trees, was not a bit happy about it.

"Stop that, you insolent thing!" roared the king of the jungle. "Stop that this instant, or I'll make a meal out of you!"

The ape was not a bit frightened by this prospect and said, "Hah! What can you do against me, Mr. Lion? I'm way up here in the trees, and you're way down there on the ground. You can't climb, and I won't come down. So, there!"

And the silly ape continued to make sport of the lion.

Unlucky for him, though, just then the tree branch he was prancing on gave way, breaking in two and sending the clownish, prankish old ape sailing downward. He fell between the lion's eager paws.

"Hah! He who laughs last, laughs loudest!" roared the lion. "Now, I'll teach you to make fun of me, Mr. Ape! I'm going to eat you up! Yes, indeed, that is exactly what I'm going to do! First though, I'll go and get a friend to help me enjoy this triumphal feast!"

And with that, the lion took the ape by the scruff of his neck, and hoisting him so, carried him to the mouth of a nearby cave and imprisoned him there behind a rock.

The ape was frantic with fear, and said to himself, "Oh heavens, whatever shall I do now?" Lucky for him, his bad fortune suddenly turned, and trotting along came the wolf, who was renowned as a bit of a fool.

Hearing Mr. Ape inside the cave, Mr. Wolf put his snout to the opening and asked, "Mr. Ape, why are you carrying on so?"

Mr. Ape was very shrewd and, sensing his chance to save his life, said, "Oh, I'm not crying; I'm just delighting in all of this food I have hidden here. You see, I'm waiting for Mr. Rabbit to come back with his kin, and we are going to fall to feasting again. We've already eaten twice as much as we need, and there's still plenty left! Oh, Mr. Wolf, I wish you could come back here in this cave and help us enjoy all of this good food!"

Well, Mr. Wolf was a notorious glutton, and so, his jaws slavering and dripping, he rolled back the stone, expecting to see a huge, bountiful feast laid out before him.

He got the surprise of his life though, for, instead, Mr. Ape popped out of the dark hole, ran between his legs, shoved him inside the cave, and rolled the stone back. That way, he managed to trap Mr. Wolf in the cave.

Then he ran away, cackling to himself. He took to the trees, exulting in his own cleverness.

Well, when Mr. Lion and his friend returned, he was quite upset to find not Mr. Ape, but Mr. Wolf, cowering behind the stone.

"Bah! We've been cheated somehow. Ah well, I suppose if we can't eat the ape, we'll just have to eat Mr. Wolf here."

And so they did.

Never let your greed get the better of you.

(Source: African fable)

The Turkeys and the Wildcat

Once, the wildcat had captured the hare and was about to devour the furry little thing, when the clever hare piped up, saying, "Oh, Mr. Wildcat, please don't eat me! I wouldn't make more than a mouthful for you anyway." And then the hare thought of a brilliant plan.

"If you release me and let me live, I'll make it so that you can have all the turkeys you want!"

And the wildcat, seeing the logic of this, released the hare, and then said, "Okay, but what do I have to do?"

The hare said, "Well, for starters, just lie in the road and pretend to be dead. When I give the signal, you will spring to life, and gobble up the biggest gobbler!"

And so the wildcat did as he was told. He went and lay down in the road and pretended to be dead, while the hare went to the turkeys and said, "Our old enemy the wildcat is lying dead in the road! Come, let us do a dance about his flyblown old corpse, and we will hit him with this stick."

And so the turkeys, young and old, followed the hare out to where the wildcat lie and told them to follow his lead, do the dance, and hit the Wildcat with a stick.

"And," he told the youngest one, "don't forget to say 'get the big gobbler, get the biggest gobbler!' as you go!"

At this, a suspicious old turkey gobbled out, "Why do you want them to say that, Mr. Hare?"

And the hare said, "It is what the young men say when they are at a war dance!"

And so they all began to dance around the wildcat, and the hare hit him with a stick. Then, the hare let out a yell and exclaimed, "Get the biggest gobbler, the biggest gobbler, the biggest gobbler!"

And at hearing that, the wildcat sprang to life and devoured the entire family of turkeys. But the hare ran away and was safe.

Never let yourself be lulled into an easy trap.

(Source: Native American folktale)

48

The Boar and the Chameleon

Once, the arrogant, pig-headed boar said to the slow chameleon, "You slow old thing! I am certainly better than you, for I can run everywhere, and you must always crawl on your belly in the dust!"

To which the tricky chameleon replied, "Bah! You think you're so special! I can beat you any day! Why, do you see that hill over there?"

"Yes," said the boar quizzically. "What of it?"

"Well," said the chameleon, "I'll race you to the foot of that hill. If you beat me, I concede that you are, indeed, greater than I. If I beat you, however, you must concede that I am, in point of fact, every bit as strong and fast as you are!"

The boar thought on it a moment, and then snorted, "Deal!"

And so the two lined up side by side, and the boar stamped in the dirt, and huffed and puffed and snuffed, and rubbed his little boar hooves to warm them up and prepare, and then was off!

The tricky chameleon though, did not prepare to run. In fact, he did not run at all, but simply grabbed a hold of the Boar's tail, and rode him along until he reached, with great huffing and puffing and lots of smelly sweat, the bottom of the hill.

"Well Brother Chameleon, where art thou?"

The chameleon let go of his tail and chirped, "Oh, Brother Boar, I am right here!"

At this, the boar was greatly perplexed, for he did not see how a creature as slow-moving as the chameleon could possibly have reached the bottom of the hill before him. So he said, "Well, I concede that, indeed, you have won that race. But, I need another before we can truly decide if I am greater, or you are my equal. So, let's try it again!"

And so the stupid boar once again snorted and stamped in the dust, kicking up a cloud as he took off like a hurricane, giving it his all and going as fast as he could to the next stop in the race.

The chameleon, however, once again simply grabbed on to the boar's tail, getting a free ride all the way.

Well, the boar made it to the next stop in the race, huffing and puffing and sweating and exhausted. He called out, "Well, Brother Chameleon, where art thou?"

And the chameleon once again chirped up, "I'm right here Brother Boar!"

The boar was struck dumb with shock. However, being a creature that lived by the Law of the Jungle, he finally hung his head in shame, and said, "Okay, Brother Chameleon, you win. I concede that you are every bit as great as me."

Never underestimate an opponent because of what he appears to be on the surface. You may be in for a surprise.

(Source: African folktale)

The Terror of the Frogs

Once there were a trio of boys out in the backyard throwing stones into a pond. The pond, which was the home of a large family of young frogs, who were quite upset by the splashing and rippling caused by the little missiles as they hit the cool, calm surface of the water.

This was a terrible danger to the frogs, and the king frog jumped from the water in indignation and rage. He hopped over to the boys and croaked a loud "ribbit!" Then he said, "Ah, cruel children! Why are you so soon to take on the unjust, evil habits of your elders? I tell you: tho this game may be nothing but sport to you, it is DEATH for us!"

And so, the moral of this story is:
What may be a foolish jest for YOU, may be
DEADLY SERIOUS business for someone else.
So, act wisely and prudently, always.

(Source: Robert Dodsley)

50

A Thousand Cuts!

Once, there were two swordsmen: a big man and a small man. The big man carried a mighty scimitar and could chop a man in half with one sweep of his mighty arm through the air. The other swordsman carried only a small dagger and had never cut a man in half. Many mocked him for his size; however, few could match him for his fleetness of foot.

One day, these two swordsmen chanced to meet on the field of battle.

Finding himself on the opposite side of the conflict with the little man, the huge, hulking swordsman laughed, "Ha! I can slice a man in half with one swing of my mighty arm! I should be able to kill a mouse like you with no effort at all!"

The smaller man then thought to himself, "He may be right, but he hasn't taken into account how small and quick I am. We'll just see if it is so easy to defeat me as what he imagines."

And then he said, "You may have size in your favor, sir, but I have speed and agility working for me! Now, let us begin!"

And so they stepped forward, and the big man swung his heavy arm, but the small man was so quick, he easily dodged the swing. The big swordsman stomped his foot in frustration but came in again for a second swing.

The small man easily dodged this swing too, and, while he was ducking and bobbing and weaving about, he reached up with his dagger . . . and gave the big man a little cut. Just a little one, but deep enough to let out a trickle of blood as the great swordsman swung to and fro in frustration.

And that is how the battle went on—until far into the night.

The two men were gasping and heaving, the big swordsman realized he was bleeding from a thousand cuts that would have, otherwise, been insignificant to him. He had lost a huge amount of blood, however. He suddenly staggered, his vision going black, and, groaning, pitched face-forward into the dirt. The little swordsman, who was exhausted but otherwise unhurt, stepped forward with a grin. He poked the big man with the toe of his boot.

"Dead! So, it seems that even a mouse can outwit a giant such as yourself, if he is but quick and cunning enough!"

And so we say today, "He died the death of a thousand cuts!" to explain a situation wherein a mighty giant is felled by a snowballing of many, many small problems.

(Source: Traditional Saying)

Afterword

We hope you've enjoyed our little excursion into the world of talking animals and their doings in and out of forest and glen. We just *know* you've learned a thing or two, but, if you haven't, please GO BACK AND READ THE BOOK AGAIN! For, a fable is told not just to entertain, but to *instruct* as well. We trust our little book has filled both requirements satisfactorily.

God bless,
Tom Baker

About the Author

Tom Baker is the author of numerous books and short stories, poems, and experimental pieces, as well as an artist and experimental musician. Five of his books have been published by Schiffer Publishing, including *Midwest UFOs and Beyond, Midwest Maniacs, Indiana Ghost Folklore, Scary Urban Legends,* and *Haunted Indianapolis* with John Titchenal. He is currently working on a book of true crime, focusing on serial killers and maniacs from the Upper Midwest region. His interests range from experimental music and art to philosophy, true crime, the paranormal and the occult, silent films, surrealism, dreams, spiritualism, and other esoteric and macabre subjects. He graduated from Ball State University in 2003 and lives in Marion, Indiana.